Perspectives

Ecosystems in Trouble

Can We Save Them?

Flying Start
to Literacy®

Contents

Introduction

How do we protect our ecosystems?

An ecosystem is all the living things in a particular place, and how they depend on each other and the nonliving things in that place. Each ecosystem forms its own unique web of life.

We cannot survive without healthy ecosystems – oceans, forests, wetlands and polar ice caps keep our planet healthy, and without them, we would not survive. But human activity is damaging these precious places.

We must protect our ecosystems. How can this be done? What can you do to help?

We need healthy ecosystems

Life in the city sometimes makes it easy to forget how much we all depend on the natural world to survive, write biologists Kate Mason and Briony Norton. Food comes from the supermarket, doesn't it? No, it comes from nature.

Think about all the things you use during one day. Where did each of these things come from? How are they connected to the natural world?

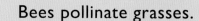

Bees pollinate grasses.

Food

To grow food, we need bees and other insects to move pollen between plants. This allows the plants to produce fruit that we can eat.

The insects that do this are called pollinators, and the number of pollinators in the world is shrinking. Honey bees (*Apis mellifera*) are an important species of pollinator and they are dying.

In some areas of China, there are no pollinators left, and people have to pollinate the plants – but humans are not nearly as good at this as bees. After all, bees and other insects have been pollinating plants for millions of years!

Cows eat grass.

Cheese and milk come from cows.

Water

Clean water is one of the most important things in our lives. Water can become unsafe when humans allow it to be polluted with industrial waste, litter, road runoff and agricultural runoff.

But nature can help us with this pollution. Forests and wetlands act like a sponge, absorbing dirty water, trapping the pollutants and then squeezing out clean water. That clean water goes into rivers and streams, which provide us with water to drink and use in other ways. All the components of these ecosystems are important in this process – from the tallest tree to the smallest bacteria in the soil.

But what happens when we lose these ecosystems? Humans have been cutting down trees and draining wetlands for many years, replacing them with farms, mines and cities. Without the forests and wetlands, it is much harder for us to find sources of clean water.

Temperature

Have you ever noticed that it's often hotter in cities than the nearby countryside? This is called the urban heat island effect. One reason for this is that there aren't as many plants in cities. When we build cities, we cut down trees and other plants – and then replace them with buildings, concrete and roads.

When cities get too hot, we end up using artificial methods, such as air-conditioning, to regulate the temperature. But this uses a lot of energy and can produce pollution and greenhouse gases.

A more natural way we can make our cities cooler places is to grow more trees and other plants. They have other benefits for cities, too. Can you think of any?

Urban heat island effect

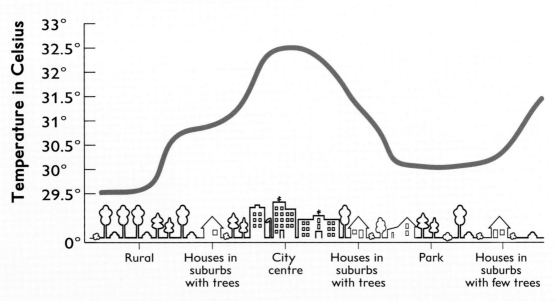

Ecosystems in danger

Why is it so important to think about long-term care for our ecosystems? asks Kerrie Shanahan.

If we can't save them all, which ones would you save? Why?

Reefs

Coral reefs are not only spectacular to look at – they are vital. They protect coastlines from erosion and damaging storms, and this protects property and saves lives.

Reefs are packed full of incredibly diverse marine animals and plants. They are home to fish that millions of people all around the world rely on as a food source. In some countries, one-quarter of all fish eaten comes from reefs.

Rainforests

Life on Earth could not survive without rainforests –
they help clean the air. Billions of trees and plants
in rainforests take in harmful carbon dioxide and
release oxygen.

Rainforests make rain. Water from the leaves of
rainforest trees and plants evaporates into the air.
Clouds form and the water inside them falls to Earth
as rain. Humans need this rain!

A huge variety of wildlife and plants live in rainforests.
Many medicines come from plants that grow in them.

Antarctica

Antarctica is unique among the continents on Earth because it's almost totally covered in ice. In fact, it comprises 90 per cent of the world's ice.

Why is this important? Because if this ice melts, ocean water levels all around the world will rise by up to six metres. This water will flood coastlines, and totally cover many islands, towns and cities.

Antarctica also has a huge influence on the world's climate and ocean systems. The white ice helps to cool the atmosphere.

Which of these ecosystems – reefs, rainforests, Antarctica – is more important than the other ecosystems?

Save the brumby . . . or not?

Wild horses called brumbies are found on the high plains in southeastern Australia. They are beautiful animals, but they are an introduced species that is damaging the ecosystem. Their numbers are out of control – they have doubled in the last five years. They have to be removed.

In this article, Joshua Hatch explores these issues: Should the brumbies be killed to preserve an important natural ecosystem? Or should they be left alone? What is the cost of not doing anything?

The brumby arrives

In 1788, a fleet of English ships carrying convicts and settlers came to Australia. Along with the people on board, there were also seven horses. For more than two centuries, descendants of those and other horses have run wild in the Australian bush, becoming feral. In the high country of southeastern Australia, these wild horses are commonly known as brumbies.

Save the brumby

Those who say the brumbies should be protected argue that the wild horses have been around for 200 years or more. They say there is plenty of land to share and that killing wild horses is inhumane.

They find the idea of destroying such a beautiful and intelligent creature is intolerable, especially when the animal was just living its life. These animals have a right to live there.

Save the ecosystem

Environmental authorities in favour of eliminating brumbies say they must be removed because the wild horses are an invasive species. They have no predators and they destroy the natural ecosystem.

Brumbies in the Snowy Mountains National Park in the Australian Alps trample the ground, compacting the dirt and making it difficult for water to seep into the soil to help plants grow. This area is an important water catchment area. It helps supply water for domestic use, agriculture, hydroelectric power and industry.

The horses also eat native plants and chew the bark off trees, leaving them prone to disease and death. When native plants die off, it becomes difficult for other native species that rely on those plants, such as rock wallabies and kangaroos, to survive, too.

The Australian Government allows other animals that have escaped into the wild to be killed: feral pigs, cats, foxes and deer, for example. But fierce debate rages over the fate of the brumbies.

The middle ground

Some argue that there's no reason to kill brumbies. They can be trapped and moved to large farms or cattle stations. There, the horses can be trained for other purposes, or just left to live out their lives without damaging the environment.

But there are too many brumbies – over 400,000 – to move them all. The effort would be impractical and too expensive. It just wouldn't work.

Should the government spend millions of dollars to try to capture and move them to new locations? What do you think is the best solution?

Children save the rainforest

It's important to protect our natural environments and the instinct to help makes sense. But is doing so too hard? After all, environmental problems are global! How could any of us possibly make a difference?

If you feel powerless to help, then this article by Carol Kim should inspire you. Maybe we can make a difference after all. What do you think?

In a classroom in Sweden, a group of young students sat, spellbound, as their teacher introduced them to the magical world of rainforests and the brightly coloured birds, poisonous frogs and monkeys that live in them. They learnt how important rainforests are in protecting the world's water supply while taking in vast quantities of carbon dioxide (a gas that contributes to global warming). Rainforests also contain plants that are used to make medicines.

The teacher explained that rainforests were being cut down and destroyed for timber and to accommodate farming. The children were only nine years old, but they were shocked. How could anyone wipe out such beautiful and important places? They desperately wanted to save the rainforests. But what could they do?

Then one boy, Roland, had an idea. "Why can't we buy some rainforest?" The idea seemed far-fetched.

"You can't just buy a rainforest!" their teacher recalled saying.

But as luck would have it, a biologist named Sharon Kinsman was visiting their classroom, and she told them that there was rainforest land in Costa Rica that could be purchased. The children immediately decided that they would buy some!

And so they began to raise money. They performed a play about rainforests and charged admission. They made and sold books and paintings. They set up cake stalls. They wrote, performed and recorded songs, and then sold CDs. They organised a fair with pony rides. Eventually, they raised over $1,600 – enough to buy 36 hectares of rainforest (bigger than 68 soccer fields).

But the effort didn't stop there. News about the children's mission spread. A television program invited them to perform their songs and a newspaper wrote an article about them. People were amazed. And motivated! Children from other schools joined the effort. The Swedish Government gave a grant of $80,000 to purchase land. A year later, more than $100,000 had been raised.

Still, the movement continued to grow – it swept the globe. "It was like a snowball," said the children's teacher, "that kept getting bigger and bigger." In the end, children from 44 countries helped raise two million dollars. Now there are about 23,000 hectares of rainforest (bigger than 42,000 soccer fields) in Costa Rica that have been purchased and are protected. Roland's idea became a reality!

After working so hard to raise money for the rainforests, the students were asked if they would like to do something for themselves and their school next.

"I am thinking about myself," one child responded. "I am thinking about my future."

Should we bring back the dingoes?

Rewilding means reintroducing animals into the natural ecosystems where they once lived. Kerrie Shanahan explains why some people believe dingoes should be reintroduced into their natural habitats. Why is the dingo important to its ecosystem? What can we learn?

The benefits of dingoes

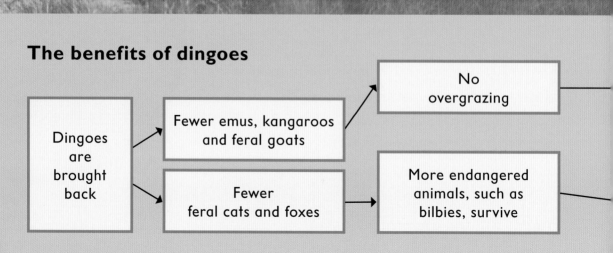

Dingoes are brought back → Fewer emus, kangaroos and feral goats → No overgrazing

Dingoes are brought back → Fewer feral cats and foxes → More endangered animals, such as bilbies, survive

Dingoes once roamed all over Australia. They were predators at the top of their food chain. When European farmers came to Australia, dingoes often attacked their livestock. Dingoes were culled and massive fences were built to keep dingoes out of vast areas of land – both farmland and natural habitats.

As a result, the population of feral foxes and cats exploded. These animals hunt native birds, reptiles and small mammals such as bilbies and bandicoots. Many native animals are now endangered.

Without dingoes, the number of large grazing animals such as kangaroos, emus and feral goats also increased. These animals eat grasses and other vegetation. They eat and eat and eat, and this overgrazing causes erosion.

To solve these problems, some people think dingoes should be brought back. What might happen if this is done?

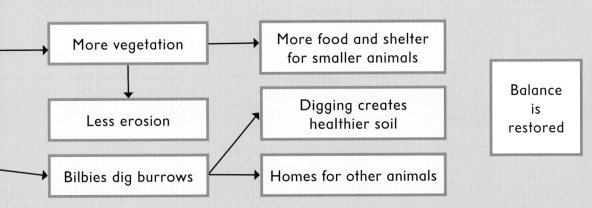

What is your opinion? How to write a persuasive argument

1. State your opinion

Think about the issues related to your topic. What is your opinion?

2. Research

Research the information you need to support your opinion.

Related *Perspectives* book   Internet   Other sources

3. Make a plan

Introduction

How will you "hook" the reader?

State your opinion.

List reasons to support your opinion.

What persuasive devices will you use?

Reason 1
Support your reason with evidence and details.

Reason 2
Support your reason with evidence and details.

Reason 3
Support your reason with evidence and details.

Conclusion

Restate your opinion. Leave your reader with a strong message.

4. Publish

Publish your persuasive argument.

Use visuals to reinforce your opinion.